1 MONTH OF
FREE
READING

at

www.ForgottenBooks.com

By purchasing this book you are eligible for one month membership to ForgottenBooks.com, giving you unlimited access to our entire collection of over 1,000,000 titles via our web site and mobile apps.

To claim your free month visit: www.forgottenbooks.com/free545645

ISBN 978-0-656-26235-9
PIBN 10545645

MANAGING END USER COMPUTING IN THE INFORMATION ERA

Thomas P. Gerrity
John F. Rockart

October 1984

CISR WP #120
Sloan WP #1595-84

Center for Information Systems Research
Sloan School of Management
Massachusetts Institute of Technology

MANAGING END USER COMPUTING IN THE INFORMATION ERA

by

Thomas P. Gerrity and John F. Rockart

Recent years have witnessed dramatic growth in the direct use of information technology as personal support tools by executives, managers and professionals. These end users, not the traditional systems development staff, are now the key forces driving the acquisition and use of computer resources. And this diffusion of computing is proliferating rapidly. Recent research finds that the growth rate in end user computing is at least five times that of conventional systems.[1] Growth rates of 50 to 100 per cent per year for end user computing are the norm today.

- o At Xerox, over 40 percent of the corporation's total computer resources are now devoted to direct support of end users. Although traditional computer "paperwork-processing" is continuing to grow, its proportional share of computer resources is steadily shrinking vis-a-vis the end user. At Xerox it is estimated that end user consumption of the computer resource will grow to 75 percent by 1990.[2]

- o Major corporate investments in personal computers are growing exponentially. One automotive company has recently ordered 25,000 personal computers. At least one insurance company, The Travellers, has two thousand personal computers installed and several thousand more on order.

o Even top executives are getting into the act. The CEO of a national restaurant chain, and his staff interrogate an on-line system to analyze trends in customer preferences, simulate changes in menu items, and do "what-if" analysis of potential price changes. The chairman of Procter & Gamble now uses a personal computer to perform his own analysis of key business situations.

As these examples illustrate, the focus of computing is shifting rapidly in organizations today.

This new period is often referred to as "The Third Era"[3] in the business use of information technology. From its early accounting and clerical applications in the First Era (circa 1955-64), the use of information technology expanded in the Second Era (1965-74) to include direct support of many operational functions in the firm (e.g., manufacturing control, order entry). With the advent of the Third Era, the relevant technology is now supporting key staff and managerial needs. Whereas the technology of earlier eras served the paperwork or data processing needs of the accountants and operational supervisors in the firm, the Third Era's end user capabilities are now focused on the information, problem-solving and communication needs of the corporation's decision makers and their staff.

Unfortunately, despite the critical importance of end user computing, th appropriate approach for managing it has not been developed in mos companies. Although much publicity has been given to its benefits, the management of end user computing is often still mired in th management techniques and processes developed during the first quarte century of the computer age; such techniques were designed to support an control a very different set of computer uses. Therefore this articl will closely examine:

o the strategic value and business impact of end user computin activities

o the pros and cons of three managerial approaches currently use to cope with end user computing

o the six key elements which we believe underlie the development o a successful end user computing strategy for the Third Era

THE VALUE OF END-USER COMPUTING

The evaluation of the benefits of end user computing is not readil amenable to the return-on-investment justifications of traditiona information systems. The initial payoffs are often in terms of th enhanced efficiency and effectiveness of an individual professional o manager. This measurement challenge is at least as great and full o qualitative judgement as is the performance appraisal process of tha same individual.

Given that the management of most organizations with widespread end use computing do not even know what most of the uses of these tools may be it is not surprising that both information systems (IS) and senio management is at least concerned, if not quite suspicious, that resource are being wasted on frivolous activities. Based on our surveys an direct observations over many years, however, we are much more sanguin about the productive uses of end user computing tools. For one thing end user professionals and managers are busy people -- they hav full-time jobs to do. So, practically speaking, they make use of this technology only where it provides a direct, quick and pragmatic benefit to getting their job done; usually by just doing some things faster and better.

Furthermore, most end users operate under normal budgetary constraints and are motivated to expend resources wisely. It is therefore startling to find some cases where a manager who has discretionary control over hundreds of thousands of dollars of spending is held suspect for a considered purchase of a three thousand dollar personal computer!

Finally, we observe in practice that another senior management fear -- that personal computers will be bought and then left sitting idle on a manager's desk -- is, in general, unfounded. Those managers whose planned use of a personal computer didn't work out are usually quite quick to get it transferred to someone who will make productive use of it. This is not to argue that there are not cases of wasted resources, or that some degree of standards, policies and guidelines is not valuable. We simply find that end users can be trusted to make sound

individual use of personal computers and similar tools to a much highe
degree than is usually suspected in top management circles.

But beyond payoffs in individual efficiency and effectiveness, we observ
in company after company that the real long term value of end use
computing lies in greatly accelerated learning on the part of the user -
about his or her job, about discovery of innovative new approaches t
tasks that actually can transform the nature of the job being done, an
finally about the new opportunities and limits of the technology itself
The growing body of end user computing experience is developing
constituency of much more sophisticated and effective "clients" of th
central IS organization than they have ever had before. And despite som
of the frictions associated with any major change, such a growin
knowledge base is ultimately to the benefit of all.

It is through this expanding organizational learning via end use
computing that the real leverage is brought to two other payoff areas fo
information technology in the Information Era:

o external competitive advantage, and

o internal organizational effectiveness.

New product/market opportunities that yield real competitive advantag
are generally spotted by professionals and managers who are "on th
firing line," close to the markets and products, and who have a
practical, working feel for new, enabling technologies. Widespread enc
user computing is developing this feel for the practical uses of
information technology at the very time that such technology offers the

greatest opportunities (and threats) in today's volatile marketplace. Hence, we believe that those firms that seize the leadership in th effective management of end user computing now are creating capabilitie to greatly increase the prospect of their being the market leaders o tomorrow.

On the other hand, as critical as they are to corporate leadership o even survival, major strategic competitive moves only come now and then. As the study of "excellent companies" shows, the factor that leads tc corporate excellence is more often the cumulative effectiveness of a vas number of minor improvements by many people than it is the "bol strategic stroke." [5] We observe that the task-related learning an discovery inherent in extended experiences with end user computinç provides a strong base for just such a set of multiple small improvements. There is a final managerial benefit: virtually every business is living in increasingly turbulent and volatile marketplaces; as uncertainty increases, the value of manageable access to gooc information also increases. Those organizations that are further up the "learning curve" in end user computing have cadres of managers at all levels with greater expertise in getting, using and disseminating gooc management information for improved organizational effectiveness. Also, to the extent that our national (and each firm's) workforce is more anc more composed of "knowledge workers" and information handlers, the leverage is even greater.

In summary, we see the effective diffusion of end user computing as a relatively low risk endeavor, kept in balance by normal budgetary controls. It is of immense potential value in developing more effective information technology clients, enhancing the prospects for achieving real competitive advantage, and contributing directly to improved organizational effectiveness. However, we also believe that time is of the essence: the leaders and laggards are being sorted out. Now is the time to select and implement effective management approaches to end user computing in the Third Era.

Current Managerial Approaches

To a great extent the rapid growth in end user demand for information resources, like those described above, has "blind-sided" many IS executives, who have been understandably myopic about this new era. For the past two decades, IS managers have been struggling just to install each new wave of increasingly productive (and complex) hardware and software. Their focus has been upon First and Second Era computing. IS staffs have been tied down by developing or enhancing these paperwork processing systems -- working feverishly to reduce development backlogs which now range from two to four years in most large companies. Available managerial time has been invested in creating better and more refined approaches to plan and control those applications which are now a steadily shrinking portion of the total information systems "pie." Despite their dramatic increase, the Third Era changes underway have not been able to receive significant time and attention from management because the demand for traditional systems has continued to grow in absolute scale. As a result, many IS executives are entering the era of end user dominance, having done very little to prepare for it. For the most part, managerial approaches to Third Era computer use have been superficial, diffuse and reactive. Separate groups have often been set up to control the use of personal computers, time-sharing and offic

systems. Most are merely _responsive_ to user-initiated demand. What i

more, IS managers are discovering that many of their critical managemen

tools and skills, developed so painstakingly over the past 25 years, ar

of little value in managing Third Era developments.

What are companies actually doing? Although the details may differ,

management usually has taken one of three general approaches to end use

computing -- monopolist, laissez-faire, or the information center.

The Monopolist Approach

Often the initial approach in many firms is for the IS organization tc

attempt to maintain firm control over all end user computing -- usually

limiting it severely.

> o For example, one consumer products company, scarred by the
>
>   painful and costly evolution of its traditional informatior
>
>   systems over the past two decades, has adopted a "go-slow"
>
>   attitude towards the integration of computers into the management
>
>   process. Not only has the firm chosen as the company standard a
>
>   complex programming language, inaccessible to all but the best
>
>   trained users, but it has also created a set of policies that
>
>   actively discourage managers from utilizing computer resources.
>
>   Each personal computer, for example, must be fully and
>
>   painstakingly justified. And personal computer users are deniec
>
>   any access to corporate databases.

There are several variations of the traditional monopolist view, but the all spring from a basic belief that the IS organization should contro all information processing: systems should be developed by professional data processing staff to ensure efficient use of compute resources, good documentation, good controls on privacy and security o data, and strong financial controls over the use of the data processin resource.

The monopolist approach is, however, breaking down in most of thos companies using it. The key reasons for its failure are as follows:

o There is not sufficient IS staff available to develop all of th needed systems. Users, faced with a two-to-four-
   year backlog, are bypassing the "monopoly" by going to external time sharing or "bootlegging" in their own small computers.

o With the cost of computer hardware declining constantly, it is becoming apparent to all that the monopolist's focus on control to maximize hardware efficiency is increasingly irrelevant.

o The documentation and controls necessary for development of larg paperwork processing systems are unnecessary for many Third Era applications, which may only be used by their authors on a one-shot basis or for a very short time.

o An increasingly computer-savvy group of young managers and staf professionals feel, and rightly so, that they can directly develop many systems more quickly and cheaply, with less friction, and more specifically targeted at their needs, than can the traditional monopoly. They refuse to place a system in the central development backlog which they know they can develop by themselves and have available much sooner. "Why should I wait eight months and pay $50,000 when I can do this over a couple of weekends on my IBM PC?" is a typical user response.

Laissez-Faire Approach

The laissez-faire approach is almost the opposite of the monopolist's view. Here, user-managers, as long as they have their own budgets, are allowed to buy whatever resources they please: time-sharing, microcomputers, and even minicomputers. This approach reflects beliefs similar to those stated by one IS manager: "No central organization can plan for end user computing. Each user is an individual with differing needs. The sum of these needs is too big, too complex, and too diverse. No single central group can possibly understand or control them all." The key here is for each user to make creative, effective use of the tools. If the corporation allows "free market" access to computation, users will spend their own budgets more wisely than a central authority could possibly do. It is, therefore, outside the role of the IS manager to worry about end user computing.

As a result of this philosophy, for example, almost half of the corporate computer resources at one of the world's largest electronics companies are now being consumed by management and staff who are developing and running Third Era systems. The corporation's posture of letting people "do their own thing" has led to a current forecasted requirement of an additional large mainframe computer every six months just to support end users. Not surprising, senior management has recently demanded reassurance that comparable benefits are being received from the increased computer costs.

In addition to financial considerations, the total "laissez-faire" philosophy has several other major drawbacks. Some are subtle, some obvious, but all are increasingly apparent. They include the following:

o There are many diverse hardware and software tools available today. Much can be gained by having a center or centers of expertise in the corporation continually studying the available tools and helping users to match their perceived needs with appropriate technology.

o The "invisible hand" reacts most strongly to the short-term tactical firefighting needs of operational managers. While these applications can be valuable, major opportunities will be missed if no one is responsible for identifying those few end user systems of most strategic benefit to the organization. These end user applications must often be targeted "top-down" without relying on the highest payoff applications being discovered "bubbling up" from individual user demand below.

o Users value on-going support. Having received advice and consulting in the appropriate hardware and software for their needs, users need continual updates in the use of the software and other aspects of end user computing. It is also ineffective to let users slowly and arduously track down the location of data specifically valuable to them, manage the transfer of data to their own systems, worry about data security and privacy, or maintain their own data bases if they are sizable. These are all matters better supported by information systems professionals.

o Efficient use of Information Era technology demands some corporate-wide standardization. Discounts are available from vendors for quantity purchases. Training programs can be run for only a small set of machinery and software -- not for each of the hundrèds of personal computers and thousands of software packages now available. Transfer of software and know-how is easier among end users using the same underlying tools. Central leadership is necessary to create an appropriately effective and evolving efficient "network architecture" to meet changing needs.

o Finally, the laissez-faire approach makes no provisions for transforming ad hoc quickly-developed support systems into formal on-going, often-used support systems. This is a task best performed by IS professionals and is increasingly seen as necessary for some Information Era systems as they gain widespread use throughout organizations.

The Information Center Approach

Recognizing the difficulties of the monopolist approach and some of the obstacles of laissez-faire, some major computer vendors, most notably IBM, have focused on an organizational approach known most commonly as the "Information Center" (IC). This initial attempt to provide a focused managerial approach toward end user computing has much to recommend it. The IC is a centrally-located group of personnel, distinct from the rest of the IS staff, to whom users can come for guidance and support concerning the selection and use of appropriate hardware, software and data.

Strong "product" expertise, education and on-going training is available from various specialist members of the IC on each supported software language and user-oriented "package" (e.g., electronic mail, word processing, graphics, and statistical analysis systems). In some cases, the IC is also charged with ensuring that each application is "justified."

o One such Information Center has been established in a major pharmaceutical company. The IC, staffed with IS support personnel, was chartered to provide assistance, upon request, with all of the 23 end user software tools that the company owned. The center's manager, however, soon found that his small staff's attempts to support the multitude of diverse users and their applications interests were highly inadequate to meet the demand. Without sufficient resources, this center was foundering. Other centralized ICs, even with a more limited range of products, have found it difficult to serve the vastly increasing number of users who desire help.The IC is the newest of the three approaches, and it is closer to providing effective results than the others. Many are quite successful. The IC, however, as usually practiced, is an incomplete management solution for the Information Era. The information center focuses

on support and, to an extent, control, of users. Both support
and control are important, but there are several shortcomings to
the usual implementation of the IC. The shortcomings are:

o The IC, as usually structured, is a centralized organization.
  Yet users desire and need localized support. [6]

o Although strong on technological and software product knowledge,
  most IC personnel often do not have the functional and
  application knowledge which is the end user's primary concern.

o The IC is a creation of the central IS department. User
  influence on its design, procedures, and services can be
  minimal. In addition, it may not even have the full backing of
  IS management, being viewed as an experimental palliative to user
  demands.

o Often the IC will represent only one or two of the four major end
  user computing technologies: time-sharing, communications
  networking, personal computers, and office systems. For
  effective end user support, all four must be managed in
  coordination.

o The IC is often only reactive to expressed user needs. Yet Third
  Era technology presents many opportunities which may not be
  recognized by technologically unsophisticated users. Proactive
  managerial efforts to identify and rank high payoff opportunities
  have been extremely useful in the organizations with which we

have worked.

o Finally and perhaps most important, the IC is an <u>organizational</u> entity -- a solution expressed in terms of organizational structure. And, structure should follow strategy. However, the majority of the firms we have seen have neglected the critical initial step -- the development of a <u>strategic direction</u> for the exploitation of Third Era technology.

A Managed Free Economy

What is needed today in many companies is a strategic approach to the management of Third Era computing. Given the potential strategic benefits to the firm, end user computing has been thrust "center stage" and demands much more than either a laissez-faire, "take what you get" approach or only limited, reactive management and support resources. Both approaches are patently inadequate because in the next few years proliferating end user computing needs will cause many major companies to spend hundreds of millions of dollars in equipment, systems development, and user time.

What is needed is a proactive and strategic approach to managing Third Era computing. This approach must balance two opposing but equally essential needs. Users must be allowed to create, define and develop their own applications of the technology to fulfill their information needs. No central organization can do this for all the diverse users in the organization -- especially in an era when almost all "knowledge workers" will soon have terminals on their desks. Yet some central authority must have the responsibility to consult with users as to what is possible and feasible, to support users where special IS expertise can add value, and to ensure that the appropriate technical policy structure is in place. The parallel to a regulated economy is very clear. Within certain reasonable and necessary guidelines and constraints, participants are free to act in their own behalf. Yet the economy is "managed" with clear strategic direction to balance the value-added to each and all.

FIVE CRITICAL ATTRIBUTES

In our various research and consulting efforts with regard to Third Era computing, we have observed or been involved with more than 50 companies. The managerial approaches to end user computing vary significantly from company to company including many variations and hybrids of the three approaches described. Some are markedly successful from both user and IS management viewpoints. Many are not. Although the exact implementations differ, those approaches considered to be successful by both users and IS exhibit all or most of the five critical attributes of the "managed free economy" approach. These critical attributes are as follows:

1. a stated end user strategy

2. a user/IS working partnership

3. an active targetting of critical end user systems and applications

4. an integrated end user support organization

5. an emphasis on education throughout the organization.

1.   A STATED END-USER COMPUTING STRATEGY

Users continually ask the questions: "What is IS going to do to support me?" "What is their end user strategy?" "What is IS management's view of the general directions of Third Era computing?" "What end user hardware and systems will be supported by IS?" "Will the specific support mechanisms (e.g., education, hardware discounts, on-going assistance) be provided?" In short, users desire a statement of strategic direction and knowledge of the key elements of its implementation.

The development of an end user computing strategy requires both an assessment of the technology and a determination of user application needs. While new products are continually being introduced, the shape of end user product direction is increasingly clear. The assessment of user needs for the future can be determined in large part by an analysis of staff department computer needs. Staffs are, after all, the major manipulators of information in the firm. And they are the focus of 80 to 90 percent of all end user computing. [7]

2.   A USER/IS WORKING PARTNERSHIP

Today, both the strategy and all programs flowing from the strategy must reflect user needs. In the past, the "rules of the game" in information systems have been formulated by the IS organization to effect efficient implementation of paperwork processing systems. These "rules" with regard to justification of systems, pricing of services, access to data, privacy, and security need to be re-examined in this new era. Because they so strongly affect end users, it is important that the new rules be worked out in collaboration with end users and their management.

o At Gillette, a set of policies and guidelines very different from those previously governing Eras One and Two have been developed to support end user computing. The key to their development is a policy group including end user departments and several senior managers from these departments. The policy committee is chaired by a user manager. While significant expertise is added to the committee's deliberations by IS, the policies which evolve are clearly seen to reflect the needs of users.

3. ACTIVE TARGETING OF CRITICAL END-USER SYSTEMS AND APPLICATIONS

Allowing ideas for uses of the new technology to merely "bubble up" from individual users is not enough. Individual managers are noticeably short-range and "local" in their thinking. Systems with long-range benefits, which span multiple individuals or departments, or which require special technological expertise to envision and formulate will not often be generated from end users alone. To ensure that limited IS resources are used well, leading companies are forcing a strategic business-oriented scan of critical end user applications now enabled by the new technology.

o At Southwest Ohio Steel, the senior management team engaged in a Critical Success Factors-based study of corporate information needs. [8] Emerging from the study was the recognition that Third Era technology could be most effectively used to provide, among other things, an information database of marketing data. This marketing database is now being accessed daily by officers and managers of the firm including Jacques Huber, marketing vice president.

4. AN INTEGRATED END-USER SUPPORT ORGANIZATION

The skills necessary to assist end users are vastly different from the skills required to design and program systems in the IS organization. First, end user support personnel must be focused on end use, not on technology. Second, as support personnel providing expert advice, not only must they be knowledgeable in a wide spectrum of new tools and techniques, but also they must have the desire and the skills to teach and help, not to do. Working with users requires patience and interpersonal skills not commonly found in traditional IS personnel. In determining the form of the Third Era central staff organization, even more important than the skill requirements is the need for that organization to have a separate identity. Much hard work is required to develop the elements of an end user strategy. In addition, ongoing user support is essential. If user support is merely a secondary function of the regular IS organization, any crisis in conventional processing can steal significant resources away from the Third Era tasks. A focus on ongoing support must be maintained or users lose confidence. To maintain this focus, separate, dedicated organizations have been formed in each of

the leading companies. Although we expect that this organization will
eventually evolve and merge with other parts of the information systems
organization, its specialized role appears to demand organizational
separation today.

    o At Gillette, all aspects of end user computing are under the
       direction of one senior manager in IS. Policies, guidelines, and
       strategic directions are well thought through and advertised.
       Experts are available from this central staff to consult about
       timesharing products, personal computers, and office systems.

However, end users are busy people. To most effectively support them,
the support person must be local, physically close by, available, and
able to speak the users' language about their business needs. [9]

    o At Owens-Corning Fiberglas, Paul Daverio, vice president for
       information systems, has transferred special IS personnel into
       the staff departments responsible for finance, personnel, etc.
       This was done to provide end user consulting onsite.

    o At Texas Instruments, end users in each department or division
       can make use of three levels of support. First, and most
       effective, are the home-grown functional specialists in the
       department. These are finance, marketing or other users who have
       become the local, very available computing experts. They, in
       turn, are supported by IS computing consultants who have more
       overall computing knowledge and a set of guidelines as to the
       attributes of applications which should be executed either via

personal computers, time-sharing, or office systems hardware and software. Referrals can be made, if necessary, to the appropriate specialty hardware or software experts. What is more, with a single IS person as a focal point for all the user specialists, knowledge about the entire end user environment in each organization can be more effectively consolidated for shaping the evolving end user computing strategy.

5. AN EMPHASIS ON EDUCATION THROUGHOUT THE ORGANIZATION

End user technology today is coming to market in extraordinary diversity. IS personnel themselves, are often uneducated. We find that less than one in ten of the IS systems analysts today have more than a cursory acquaintance with the new end user technology. Senior management, in general, is not adequately informed. And middle management, deluged with an extraordinary number of claims by vendors and uncertain of what moves to make, needs increased understanding of the ways in which the technology can be best applied to particular tasks. A well-thought-out educational program, adapted to the needs of each type of "student" is absolutely necessary today to allow an organization to make effective use of the technology.

o At ARCO, this opportunity is being met head-on. A ten-day program has been devised and instituted to re-educate 1000 of the company's top IS personnel. The course centers on the concepts, tools, and techniques of the Third Era. In addition, short seminars are being given for the very senior management of the corporation stressing both basic concepts and current, effective uses of the new technology within ARCO. Courses for middle management are being developed as well.

CONCLUDING THOUGHTS

The recent dramatic increase of end user computing at all levels within organizations offers major opportunities for business value: it can provide enhanced possibilities for using information technology for competitive advantage, for discovering and implementing many operational efficiencies, and for enhanced managerial effectiveness. However, in order to reap these benefits, senior management must avoid the pitfalls of technology-focused approaches and ensure the development of a business-driven strategy for managing end user computing.

Ours is an era when astute leadership in exploiting information technology will create a competitive edge in the marketplace. Yet, fearing that they will lose control over computing costs, many managers hesitate to pursue the substantial benefits offered by end user computing. Before the end user era, an analysis of the costs and benefits of each major proposed application system or hardware purchase was possible through careful scrutiny of the IS budget. Today, however, such single-point control is no longer possible; usage is widely scattered throughout the organization -- and in much smaller increments.

But adequate control over computer utilization is feasible today. Ensuring that the five attributes cited above are in place will produce a working partnership between line management and IS staff, who together can implement two quite different but complementary forms of "control" over the computing environment.

As a first and vital step, a set of policies, standards, and guidelines must be developed. These will ensure a standard technical and management environment. Such an environment can yield significant benefits such as the availability of volume hardware and software discounts from vendors and the ability to mount education programs and assistance for a limited set of standard products. In addition, it gives users the ability to move freely from one part of the organization to another without needing to learn a new set of hardware and software systems. All users will be assured that their personal computers "connect" to the network, allowing access to one another and to remotely stored data.

With guidelines in place, individual end user projects of size must be scrutinized to ensure they have business value. The responsibility for this control belongs with the local unit's line management. Therefore, line management must increasingly be knowledgable of the potential value of technology -- at least to the extent necessary to determine whether expenditures on computers or communications makes good business sense. Such knowledge requires, as we have already noted, that these managers receive education in technology. IS can and should be consulted for advice in specific instances, but the basic control over what is being done -- in an era when virtually everyone in the corporation will soon have a terminal -- has shifted from the staff experts to the line or

References

1. Rockart, John F.; Flannery, Lauren "The Management of End User Computing," Communications of the ACM, Volume 26, Number 10, October 1983, pp. 777 - 784.

2. Benjamin, Robert I. "Information Technology in the 1990's: A Long Range Planning Scenario," MIS QUARTERLY, Volume 6, Number 2, June 1982, pp. 11-31.

3. Rockart, John F.; Scott Morton, Michael S. "Implications of Changes in Information Technology for Corporate Strategy," INTERFACES, Volume 14, Number 1, January-February 1984, pp. 84-95. Also, Rockart, John F. "Role of the Executive in Information Management," Global Technological Change: A Strategic Assessment, Proceedings of a Symposium for Senior Executives, MIT, June 21-23, 1983.

4. Keen, Peter G. W.; Scott Morton, Michael S. Decision Support Systems: An Organizational Perspective, Addison-Wesley Publishing Company, Inc., Reading, Massachusetts, 1978. Also, Rockart, John F.; Treacy, Michael E. "The CEO Goes On-Line," Harvard Business Review, Volume 60, Number 1, January-February 1982, pp. 82 - 88.

5. Peters, Thomas J.; Waterman, Jr., Robert H., In Search of Excellence, Harper & Row, New York, N.Y., 1982.

6. Op. cit., Rockart and Flannery, p. 783.

7. Ibid, Rockart and Flannery, p. 779.

8. Rockart, John F. "Chief Executives Define Their Own Data Needs," HBR, March-April 1979, pp. 81-93. Also, Rockart, John F.; Crescenzi, Adam "Engaging Top Management in Information Technology," Sloan Management Review, Summer 1984, Volume 25, Number 4.

9. Withington, Frederic G., "Coping with Computer Proliferation," HBR, May-June 1980, pp. 152-164.

CPSIA information can be obtained
at www.ICGtesting.com
Printed in the USA
BVHW04*1202060818
523683BV00013B/135/P

9 780656 262359